Wild Brujeria

by Tatiana Maria Corbitt

Curious Corvid Publishing

Wild Brujeria by Tatiana Maria Corbitt

© 2024, Tatiana Maria Corbitt

All rights reserved.

Published in the United States by
Curious Corvid Publishing, LLC, Ohio.

No part of this publication may be reproduced, stored in a retrieval system, stored in a database and / or published in any form or by any means, electronic, mechanical, photocopying, recording or otherwise, without the prior written permission of the publisher, except as permitted by U.S. copyright law.

Cover Art by Mitch Green

ISBN: 978-1-959860-30-3

Printed in the United States of America

Curious Corvid Publishing, LLC

PO Box 204

Geneva, OH 44041

This is a work of fiction. Unless otherwise indicated, all the names, characters, businesses, places, events and incidents in this book are either the product of the author's imagination or used in a fictitious manner. Any resemblance to actual persons, living or dead, or actual events is purely coincidental.

www.curiouscorvidpublishing.com

First Edition

"Brujas are the new generation of spiritual activists and teachers and healers. The Spanish word for witch is not simply a straightforward translation of the English. *Bruja* ('*brew-ha*') is the word for "female witch", and *brujo* means "male witch", but the terms connect to different histories than that of the Anglo-Saxon witch. They instead refer to the traditions of West Africa that made their way to the Caribbean and the Americas through slavery, and to the traditions of the Indigenous peoples of the Americas, who were displaced and forced to assimilate to the cultures of European colonizers...

Brujas are born in the US. They are born in the Caribbean. They are born in Mexico, in Central America, in South America. Their skin is brown, red, yellow, white. They speak Spanish and Creole and Nahuatl. They are female. They are male. They are gender nonconforming. They are queer. They are Catholic. They reject Catholicism. They have ancestors of Yoruba. They were brought up with Indigenous wisdom. They have been disconnected from their homelands. They feel a calling to magic, so they reach for what they can. There's one thing they all have in common: the power of their ancestors, which runs through everything they touch."

- Dr. Lorraine Monteagut, *Brujas: The Magic and Power of Witches of Color*

Table of Contents

- wild brujeria 2
- a letter to myself 3
- heritage 6
- burn me 7
- letter to my first girlfriend 10
- they won't have us 13
- alienated 16
- dissociation 17
- friends of the thorns 20
- this house is burning 21
- watch your son 23
- the narcolepsy fog 26
- college friends 28
- empathy 29
- tread softly 31
- aestivation 33
- wonderland 35
- sweet treats 37
- a letter to home 40
- mexican mocha 42
- renaissance days 44
- i learn of my father as I learn of myself 46
- crucify me 47
- impermanence 49
- careless 51
- how small can i get? 53
- dragon slayer 56

- from the borderline lover 57
- my father's child 59
- resurrection 61
- human monster 64
- on community 65
- on leaving before you do 67
- earth wisdom 70
- this end, a race 72
- true lies 73
- forswear me not 75
- breakthrough 77
- queer 79
- portland tears 82
- sunshine tea 83
- mother tree 85
- your words cannot hold me 87
- microaggressions 89
- just breathe 91
- asleep in the Shakespeare garden 93
- ghost people 95
- to the last therapist I'll ever date 97
- i love myself better than you ever did 99
- i'm staying 101
- moon blood 103
- beware of fire 105
- on running away 108
- songbird 109
- come with me 111

- empty lips sink ships 113
- on my fourth disability claim denial 115
- you cannot name me 117
- a letter to my ancestors 119
- bleed us dry 121
- i was born whole 123
- worthy of tenderness 125
- always home 127
- narcolepsy, the thief 130
- narcoleptic warrior 131
- never truly alone 133

Wild Brujeria

They call me 'bruja'

Because I flew too close to the sun

And now its rays spill from my mouth,

And the moon spills from mine eyes.

They called me 'witch'

And strung me up for speaking truths

About unwanted hands on innocent skin.

They tried to burn me

With flames of eternal damnation

Licking my ankles.

I became ash and floated away

To the edges of this globe,

Arose within a new form, in a new city.

They call me 'bruja'

For good reason:

I am the universe embodied,

Magick, transformation,

Dark and light all in one.

I call myself 'bruja'

Bruja

Brujita

You deserved better.

WILD BRUJERIA

The earth and moon and stars
Are your family now.

- *wild brujeria*

Wild Brujeria

They're stronger than they know.

If I had to cast a wager, I'd bet on them every time.

They are the sea, the mountain, the tributary itself.

In our darkest times, they were there for me,

Protecting me

    Holding me

        Feeding me

            Bleeding for me

They will always fight for me.

In them, I am never alone.

Together, we are whole

- a letter to myself

WILD BRUJERIA

Wild Brujeria

My grandma always told me

To scrub my elbows.

The Mexican in me

leaks out from my creases,

staining my skin brown

in unlikely places.

I noticed my brown-bruised knees, armpits, groin,

All conjoined,

I saw myself as a whole

but my white family saw me in

pieces–

coconut sunscreen slathered thick.

"Get your elbows," my grandma said,

"You don't want them any darker."

No, grandma, *You!*

don't want them any darker.

I could bleach my skin,

but I'd still be Mexican,

maybe you'd like my elbows then, but,

my essence remains

       no matter my color

meaning everywhere I go,

    I am the "other".

        - heritage

Wild Brujeria

Cremate me.

Don't let me grow old and rotten,

Burn me while I'm still beautiful,

My cheeks still rosy,

My womb intact.

Don't let them crack me open

And rip out my meat,

Sew my eyes closed,

Screw my mouth shut –

No.

Let me burn while I'm still me.

Don't preserve me like a doll – cold and unblinking.

I am a shooting star, streaking, brilliant,

Don't let them win in the end.

Burn me.

- burn me

WILD BRUJERIA

Wild Brujeria

The only gems I need

Are those nestled and gleaming on leafy boughs.

My diamonds are a play of shadow and light

When the fresh morning dew

Plants a kiss upon a pink rosebud.

The sun ignites the bead,

Gasoline to a flame

To create this luxurious treasure

For me and only me.

Is that enough for you, though?

The peony you held on our first date,

That is my love language.

I can't afford the things they tell us we should want

But I can take you outside,

Offer you sun-ripe wild raspberries–

Clustered rubies hidden in thorny brambles,

Symphonies of warbling birds,

Emerald leaves that cleanse the air we breathe.

WILD BRUJERIA

All these and more can be yours too,
Will my treasures be enough for you?

- letter to my first girlfriend

Wild Brujeria

Who do I think I am?

To have this body, a womb,

and to want more for myself

than to create new consciousness,

new souls for society to suck –

to sell more Nikes and college degrees,

to have more debt, so they can have more, what?

drink up the water that's drying?

eat up the land that's dying?

I always wanted to be more

than a vehicle and a flesh servant

to innocent bundles I could never protect.

Not really, when

our very air makes us sick,

and, god forbid, I have a girl

whose body is never hers

but is a continent to be conquered,

a land to be razed.

I can't even protect my own body

or those of my friends.

1 in 3 women have been sexually assaulted

yet, somehow, so has every woman I know.

Wild Brujeria

The system that is supposed to protect us,

serve justice, instead exploits us,

and you ask me to bring

more life into this?

No, I refuse – you can try to force me, but,

even if I have to use a coat hanger,

I will RIP that seed of life from me.

They will not have us, not in the end.

I could never, in good conscience,

peer into the delicate face of a newborn

knowing what I'm bringing them into,

knowing the ache of whiteness, brownness,

everything-in-between-ness,

knowing that I'd not only pass on

my indignation, but also

my compliance.

Creation myths claim God planted life

into the belly of the Earth –

bringing forth life instantly.

What they got wrong is

God is Mother Earth

and she needed no man!

Wild Brujeria

She squatted and brought forth nations.

Life is not conception.

It is born in agony – ripping – stretching –

living through an event of blood, sweat,

and a sweet afterbirth,

proof that you can survive more than you think.

I turn myself inside out

to bring forth my art

something that will outlive me,

but I won't crack myself open

to bring forth life

knowing what it does to someone–

to be forced to live it here.

- they wont have us

Wild Brujeria

Wild Brujeria

My first poetry reading

I sat once where you do,

Yet I was in a different world,

A fish out of water.

But now I have the mic

I'm deaf – you couldn't tell?

Hard of hearing, whatever you wanna call me.

What matters is, I'm an alien.

I live here on your planet,

I even speak your language,

I sit where you sit –

While the crowd is in awe of verbal poetry

Swept up together in communal feeling,

I am lost in the waves of uncatchable vowels.

Consonants are my puzzle pieces

And if I can't see your mouth,

I CAN'T HEAR YOU.

I am always alone –

Never hearing enough to be here,

And my beautiful new language,

The language of sign,

The language of accessibility for me and my people

WILD BRUJERIA

Is nowhere to be found.

I'll be fully deaf by the time I'm forty,

That's what the doctors say

Will my world be accessible by then?

Or will I die like so many before me –

Deprived of language, community, life itself?

- alienated

Wild Brujeria

Frozen fingers on moss

Tickle, tease, play

A soft touch, a warm caress

Flesh, bone, and bark

A symphony of matter, itself

Roots spring from the ground, to my feet

Though I tap my toes to count the time

It passes through me like a shiver

A mushroom with rings on rings

Munches happily on the tree surface

Does it hurt? I wonder

To be consumed, inch by inch

I should know by now

The numbness kicks in, eventually,

Deadens me to death's grip

Even if I can't escape

I am not there

Anymore

- dissociation

Wild Brujeria

Wild Brujeria

Did you know

The gum you stuck in my hair,

The valentine of mine you tore to pieces,

The sneers

The sighs

All them hillbilly lies

Tied a cord around my throat

So tight I couldn't speak?

My lips grew rose buds

Amongst the thorns that held them shut.

I kept to myself

To protect myself –

But true solitude consumes the soul

One empty day at a time.

Today, I offer my fully bloomed roses

To friends of the thorns.

We loosen each other's bonds

Ripping stitches, one by one,

Wild Brujeria

Our voices may be groggy,
But our work is never done.

- friends of the thorns

WILD BRUJERIA

I could bleach my skin in acid,

Melt my flesh to the bone,

Yet your hands would still linger,

Haunting this body I was born in.

They say I drank too heavily,

Danced too prettily.

I locked myself behind a door.

I still hear the sound of the knob:

Turning

Turning

Turning

This house is burning.

- this house is burning

WILD BRUJERIA

WILD BRUJERIA

I told you what happened to me

before my body let my brain register my body.

I told you what he did to me,

his hands urgent, grabbing more

of what wasn't his.

You asked me why there was alcohol,

why I was dancing,

you never asked if I was okay.

I wasn't okay.

I am still not okay.

If I screamed, "he finger-fucked me!"

You'd respond with, "Watch your mouth!"

I know this already —

you're more angry at me for saying it,

than at him for doing it.

- watch your son

Wild Brujeria

Wild Brujeria

I keep opening my notebook

as if I have something to say.

It's between fogs

of sleep, wake, war, love,

that I lost my lips

amongst sinking ships,

between the lines lie the answers to all our prayers.

Lord God,

Let me get some deep sleep,

but not deep enough

to fall back into my nightmares.

I have more friends to see

within me

than I do without

without

      without

           without

peeping eyes I am free

but if a tree

falls

      and no one hears it,

WILD BRUJERIA

does the tree know

    it fell silently?

- the narcolepsy fog

WILD BRUJERIA

They went slow, took their time
smelled the flowers, drank them too.
I stayed home burning electric into the night,
now I am utterly spent like the bulbs and they
are making butter money,
with their butter hands,
out of a butter life.
I thought I was good enough to be them.
I thought what made me different
also made me strong.
Instead, I'm twenty-five with crumbling teeth,
dental care is not for the poor
in a society where the lack of money
makes you unworthy of care.
They turn around and say, "you could be here!
If you work hard enough!"
My father is the hardest worker I know.
He's been poor his whole life.
Tell me, friend, what work have you done?
To get where you are
with your foot at my throat?

At least now I know
I can survive without you.

- college friends

Wild Brujeria

Willow tree, I give to thee

this, my dear sweet melody,

first there's you and then there's me,

Dig deep your roots, show me the key

to flourish as if life were free.

If I could reach into my bones,

in between my painful moans

I'd revel at the rigidity –

how close you are – you are in me.

Say you fall and mushrooms grow

between your spine, both high and low,

a garden of life begins to show

in death we are equal, that I know.

A cut on flesh will draw forth blood,

A cut on bark will ooze a mud.

Who am I to say

Pain hurts only me?

I certainly don't claim to have

the only eyes that can see.

- empathy

WILD BRUJERIA

Wild Brujeria

Tiptoe softly.

Don't disturb the moss,

the trees need their sweaters.

Tread carefully.

Watch out for slugs

and their slow, soft bodies,

one misstep - and SPLAT -

they're gone forever.

Tiptoe softly.

Leave earth better

than you found it.

- tread softly

Wild Brujeria

Wild Brujeria

My voice scares people.

I see their flinches

as my truths begin to spill,

and I am hung up in the thrill

of freedom in my chest walls.

Is it the steel quake in my voice?

From all those years it spent shoved

beneath the surface

not desiccating, but

aestivating –

like the lung fish

in dry soil.

- aestivation

Wild Brujeria

Wild Brujeria

Falling in love with you,

your ocean eyes

and true lies

(how could you love someone like me?)

I fall,

keep falling,

down the rabbit hole.

But with each embrace,

we must once again, separate,

our kisses are beautiful, but

never eternal.

The closer I get to you,

our inevitable goodbye –

grows that much more tragic.

- wonderland

Wild Brujeria

Wild Brujeria

Neon yellow fingernail paint,

a pile of yellow M&Ms

tempting me to BITE

but not everything is

what you hope it to be.

Couldn't I spend a buck or two

on a delicious treat?

I'm a child

in an adult's body

but I limit myself by

not allowing myself savor

the flavors

of life.

A hard, candy shell,

chocolate, creamy sweetness inside.

- sweet treats

Wild Brujeria

Wild Brujeria

I hold memories of us in my hands

Though I want to let go.

My fingers clench, unwilling,

It's chilling

How much I want you back,

Even if it's just to hurt me again.

Last time I was home

You threatened to call the police on me

For wanting a conversation,

For using my big-girl voice.

Long before,

I'd shoved it down, deep into the ground,

Where the moss refuses to grow

And the worms slide their slick, wet bodies.

I hid my voice in the trees,

In the birds, in the bees,

All those years spent on my knees

Worshiping a god that I couldn't please.

I still have nightmares of you

Kicking me out to the street.

I walked away, head high, heart in flames,

These days, it's all I dream about.

Wild Brujeria

I know your dreams died when mine did too.

I had to find a new dream,

I had to start anew.

I won't bear a man's children,

I won't graduate from medical school,

And if my last two degrees weren't enough for you,

I doubt another would crack open your heart,

Pour out all that love and acceptance

That I needed growing up.

Fruits have seeds, and we have none,

Only weeds, and reeds,

And unmet needs.

- a letter to home

Wild Brujeria

I could lay my skin bare,

Show the edges of my bones

Spin sex, breathe into your loins

A soft sea breeze, a powerful wave

with crashing and commotion.

You'll love it, drink me in,

First with your eyes, then

With your mouth.

I share my fairy light with you

So ubiquitous and mysterious

But you cast it away –

You say you want more than sex,

Is that all it was, to you?

My essence, wispy as spun candy floss

Sweet, but melts at the first touch of a tongue...

Where were you?

I didn't just give you sex,

I gave you my world

Packaged with kisses and bliss,

Dark as cacao,

Spicy as cayenne,

Energizing as black coffee–

A Mexican mocha...
Too exotic for your taste.

- mexican mocha

Wild Brujeria

It's time for me to go to bed,

But what about all this shit in my head?

Boxes brimming with knick-knacks and scarves,

Whistles, and bells, a knife that carves,

There are teddy bears

And longing stares,

Ice cold mugs

Full of beer suds,

Gelato and a horse's gallop,

That one beating that packed a wallop,

Overgrown hedges,

My favorite pair of wedges,

There she sits, snug as a bug

Between ice cream

And

Sunscreen,

Don't slip away, my love,

Like everything else,

In my heart, the sun shines on you forever

Let us stay –

WILD BRUJERIA

Soak up its rays

Until the very end of our days.

- renaissance days

Wild Brujeria

I'm an October baby

But my father was born in November.

His mother labored alone that Halloween night.

His father was spilling blood on foreign soil

While his mother was spilling blood, innards, and my father on a hospital floor.

I never knew these grandparents,

I only know them between the lines of details I've gleaned about them.

This chilling autumn scene sets the stage for the rest of the show.

My father hated his birthday being directly after Halloween,

He got stale candies and cakes painted in neon orange and midnight black.

He never told me directly,

But one time I asked if he'd like a Halloween party for his birthday

And his skin took on a vampiric pallor –

As if some light had been snuffed out of him.

My father is the kind of man to hang himself up at night next to his coat

He isn't someone used to having preferences –

The prerequisite to having dreams.

But there they exist, within him, still.

If only he knew himself,

Then I could know him too.

- i learn of my father as I learn of myself

Wild Brujeria

Arizona was my home,

My ancestors' too,

Mexican and pioneer, alike.

How I miss the dry

Baking heat,

The Sonoran desert,

Cacti, road runner, clear blue sky.

It comes back to me in pieces,

Floating, ash in the wind,

Dusty trails, sand in shoes,

Desert camping with Grandpa.

He points out to me

The crucifix tree,

Thorned branches like those on Christ's head

In the end

"Everything out here will stick, sting, or poke ya."

Is it possible

We loved it even more

Because of the pain?

- crucify me

Wild Brujeria

Wild Brujeria

Flames consume as they lick,

Tenderly tearing apart cells all at once,

Combust,

Slip a heavy finger along the seams of matter

And ripppppp –

Until there is nothing left before you,

Nothing behind you,

Just smoke and ash.

Rubble of a world left behind.

No tears to wipe –

There's no one left

To mourn.

- impermanence

Wild Brujeria

Wild Brujeria

I killed a fly today,

The small kind that likes my food,

I didn't want him in my greens.

Though I feigned hitting him earlier,

This time I struck –

With animal aggression – MINE

A small part of me knew I'd regret it

And I did as soon as my hands closed –

Opened, hoping he was miraculously alive –

But knowing in my heart he was dead.

There his fragile body lay

Until I blew it away.

- careless

Wild Brujeria

Wild Brujeria

Ribs on chest,

Ribs in mirror

Stretch them like

An accordion.

My organ walls on display;

Sternum, sharp, hinges

To a beaded shoulder

Bare as a summer's day.

I keep wondering

How small I can get,

How close to

The essence of things.

- how small can i get?

Wild Brujeria

Wild Brujeria

Burnside bridge at 9am,

clear, cerulean sky,

boats bobbing in the Willamette

passersby, some smiles too –

And then there's you,

far off,

the size of three seagulls stacked

and watching us,

middle finger out, jabbed

towards me.

Was I smiling too prettily?

In my short hair cut, crop top, and Docs?

From fury to frenzy,

a twisted smile, and

a Damascus blade

you hold it low, away

from traffic

so only I could see

you would love to cut me,

this soft, supple body of mine...

How could he?

Your advance continues –

Wild Brujeria

I could tear my eyes away and run,

but where? Jump into the river?

Or traffic?

No, I've faced bigger monsters than you.

Monsters that hug you,

make you feel safe,

Monsters that destroy your faith.

You could tear my body apart

But never my heart.

My blade was longer than yours,

and that scared you off,

Or was it my stance?

the look in my eye

begging you to let me use it?

Let me slay the dragon

once and for all.

- dragon slayer

WILD BRUJERIA

Every moment I don't hear from you

I wonder what I did wrong,

Why I'm not good enough,

Not

good

Not good enough

Not good

Enough

Lay me down against fragile soil,

Teach me to believe again.

- from the borderline lover

Wild Brujeria

Wild Brujeria

I find myself asking,

why doesn't my dad like me?

A strange child I was, yes, but

That was enough

To drive him away?

- my father's child

Wild Brujeria

Wild Brujeria

How long does it take to restart a heart?

Before my arteries, my veins collapse?

Whisper to myself,

everything's okay

And hope,

maybe,

it will be, someday

- resurrection

Wild Brujeria

Wild Brujeria

Silver blade to a feathered throat,

I don't want to hurt the poor thing

But

"They were bred for this."

And there it sits,

Tail up in the death-cone

And there's the blade in my hand,

But it's not my hand anymore

And this is not a bird

And I am not a human

The hand in front of me saws through

The soft feathers, then skin, tendon, bone –

Blood spurt.

I am forever stained red

And as this poor bird bled,

It watched me with a question, hanging,

Until its eyes went blank,

Lost forever

To the nothingness.

WILD BRUJERIA

I could have wept, but instead
I went on to the next.

- human monster

WILD BRUJERIA

Take my hand,

Let us

Ring-round the rosy

The void inside fills

At being seen,

One drop of sand at a time

The hourglass of life

Is more full

With you here.

Let us forage

Mushrooms and shiny things

From each others' hearts,

Fill that little red basket

And float away

Together

Or apart,

We may hold this moment

Forever in our heart.

- on community

Wild Brujeria

Wild Brujeria

Our first argument

(If you could call it that)

I thought I lost you.

You saw me pull away,

Drop your hands

So as to hold mine

From intertwined,

To a single vine.

You saw the steel at my core

(Not the part that wants more –)

The diamond backing to my bones,

The part that survived the sticks and stones

Clung to life when I'd rather not.

The part that stayed when I thought I should rot,

Thank God I saw your fear

Mirrored in mine own

And stopped myself

From losing that home.

- on leaving before you do

Wild Brujeria

Wild Brujeria

I visited my tree friend,

An evergreen with eyes on the bark.

We've been friends ever since

I cut the English Ivy choking its body

Digging microscopic holes into its skin

Wounds for disease to enter

No more –

Thanks to my trusty pearl-handled stiletto blade.

Today, they asked me

Why I need money for food

When food is all around

(they found the concept of a grocery store strange)

I was baffled, my immediate answer,

"It's just how it is, I don't know why,"

But I did know why,

A secret so loud that if I whispered it to life,

It'd take on a new form,

Become a cry for help,

A herald for change –

A target at which to aim

Too much for my tiny human brain.

- earth wisdom

Wild Brujeria

It's the end of the book,

You've turned the last page

Bergamot, lavender, sage

Mists the air,

A sordid affair

And the king ran away with his mage.

I could sit here and write

A soliloquy on flight,

Bemuse over light-winged birds

That, in their fright,

All at once, do alight

Whisking autumn,

A shiver,

A quiver,

A clenching of pearls.

Dear one, you've left

Like all things must,

But in your wake

My palate tastes dust.

I long, this winter,

For a warm hand to hold,

Wild Brujeria

I make up for the cold

This white, shivering, mold

Begging for a bow

From the bandstand,

Mugs full of steaming tea

And sweet, dark, coffee

Keep my hands warm

Give me a handle to hold

To brace,

For this end, a race.

- this end, a race

Wild Brujeria

"No one will ever love you

As much as I do,"

Said my mother to tiny-me...

It's no wonder I fear to be seen,

Why I feel so unlovable,

Why I'm more comfortable

Being second-place

Than embraced

In the spotlight.

"No one will love you

As much as I do,"

My mother told me as a child.

Back then, I was wild

Like spring flowers and baboons—

Why would anyone love me?

I was never loved enough

To be cared for properly

And apparently

I'll never get any better.

- *true lies*

WILD BRUJERIA

Wild Brujeria

To my mother

I was a horse to be broken.

My wild heart alight

With the fire of life,

Spice,

Passion,

Incongruence.

Flaming arrows may pierce me,

But I let them serve as kindling

For the blaze.

I will never regret

My wild ways.

- forswear me not

Wild Brujeria

Wild Brujeria

Why must the sparrow hop

With fear in its eyes

Avoiding the comfort

Of the feeder perch?

Instead, he gathers seed

Scattered amongst the rock and dirt,

Tussles the nuggets

Free of their shells,

Feathers quivering

At every sound of the world.

All he sees is danger,

Not the silky feather,

Nor the clean hanging seed

If only from his struggle

He could be freed.

- breakthrough

Wild Brujeria

Wild Brujeria

It used to be that we got burned at the stake,

Now they bring machine guns into our safe spaces,

Shoot down our brilliant, soft bodies,

Stardust in a dark sky –

Silence.

- queer

Wild Brujeria

Wild Brujeria

I've Summited the Mount - I'm here

Breathing in the thin atmosphere.

I glow, dripping, luminescent

Yet no one sees me at present–

Am I real?

States away from my birthplace, my home,

Further still from my ancestors

Who built temples of blood and stone.

My throne - a reclaimed dumpster chair

My sash - a plushy warm blanket

And of course, most importantly,

A strong, stable, roof above me,

I've made it, finally!

So why, then, do my lungs still burn?

And WHY do I FEEL so GODDAMN uncertain?

Parchment leaves linger from Autumn,

They flow in streams, over oily cement

In the light's glare, a rainbow lament.

I live in a grey city full of grey strangers

Whose grey eyes slide past me

They don't know I'm here, you see?

Am I real? Beats me...

Wild Brujeria

According to modern physics,

A particle is in a state of flux until it's observed;

If I fall alone in the forest, let no one be perturbed,

I won't make a sound, because I won't be heard.

Ferns dance for me though, and in doing so

They bid me their friendly hello

With stately trees and stinging bees.

But humans don't live alone in that wild,

So in the city I'll stay - a scared little child,

And maybe one day I'll be brave enough, tame enough,

To accept the rain on my face, let it stain.

It may very well take years to gain

Those permanent Portland tears -

Let it rain.

- portland tears

WILD BRUJERIA

For Sunshine Tea –

Two sprigs of sweet mint

To settle the gut,

The furnace of the soul.

Spicy ginger and vibrant turmeric,

A sunset in a mug,

A warm hug.

Don't forget echinacea,

Her downy petals

Remind us to purge

What no longer serves

Us.

A splash of honey and bright, tart lemon

Boil water and let it set

To wash away

The city's decay.

Drink one cup of tea per day.

- sunshine tea

Wild Brujeria

WILD BRUJERIA

Sleepy eyes, rest well,

You are safe here

Beneath a wise oak tree.

Rest, head, against this firm bark,

Immoveable, here just for you.

Roots beneath

    Encircle me

Sleeping beneath

    That mother tree.

- mother tree

Wild Brujeria

Wild Brujeria

Blood is thicker than water,

I'm not your son, nor your daughter.

Always alone in my type,

Always wrong, never felt right.

You took my fruit, held it ripe

In your hand and

Squeezed out its juice,

My flesh you won't choose

I am death – not your muse.

- your words cannot hold me

Wild Brujeria

WILD BRUJERIA

Every time my hair grows out,

People tell me how good it looks

long.

I keep it short

And tight,

Because it just feels right.

Still they find a way

To take that thrill

Away.

- microaggressions

Wild Brujeria

WILD BRUJERIA

You're taking a piss
Not solving world hunger

- just breathe

Wild Brujeria

WILD BRUJERIA

Juliet, asleep in the Shakespeare Garden,

Enthroned by roses above,

With thorns upon their brow.

And Romeo, oh Romeo,

Waiting for the eyes to open,

The fingers to flutter,

To hold his own again.

Dear sweet Romeo, with sweat upon your brow,

Don't leave them behind again.

- asleep in the Shakespeare garden

Wild Brujeria

Wild Brujeria

The world seems bigger and emptier without you.

When I had you,

You took up so much space

There wasn't enough room

For me to breathe.

I took your pain,

I soaked it all in

Until it became

The reason I stayed.

It makes sense you left

As soon as you came,

But ghost-people

Don't move on quite so fast.

- ghost people

Wild Brujeria

WILD BRUJERIA

I asked you

To be careful with my heart

Because I bleed too easily

I dream of knives on my skin

Pulling beads of red

Rubies

Across

I dream of nooses adorning my neck

Kissing me a sweet farewell

Yet in the end

You filled me with your poison

And dumped me over the phone

Screaming

Then texted for your book back.

If it had been anything else

I'd have torn it to pieces

But a book?

I could never

Destroy a story

As carelessly as you.

- to the last therapist Ill ever date

Wild Brujeria

WILD BRUJERIA

I want to cut you out of my skin.

Instead, I anoint it with lavender,

Cedarwood, lemongrass,

Bathing myself in the flowers

You never gave me.

- i love myself better than you ever did

Wild Brujeria

Wild Brujeria

I'm staying

Because in a few weeks

Today's tart wild blackberries

Will grow into something so sweet

I'll forget what sour

Ever tasted like

- im staying

Wild Brujeria

Wild Brujeria

It's the first phase of the moon I'll live without you

Since you ended things.

My uterus twists and turns

Burning my insides,

I'll bleed you out

From every corner

Of me.

But I haven't washed my sheets

Since we dirtied them

Together.

- moon blood

Wild Brujeria

Wild Brujeria

Red hair

The same color of fallen leaves in autumn

I thought it would keep me warm

Be a home

And a hearth

A wheel and spoke to ground my life

But

Your fire...

It consumed me.

- beware of fire

Wild Brujeria

Wild Brujeria

My town

small and green, nestled deep in the mountains,

Quiet, secluded,

With its grassy knolled trails

And lanes full of people I don't know.

They grimace at my short hair, my misalignment,

But I could ignore them and find myself in the trees

At peace with the pine needle litter,

The luxurious bodies of water

With more fish than people

Until you came and poisoned me,

Ripped my roots from the ground.

I couldn't drive past that building anymore

From whence I once escaped,

So I ran away.

I ran states away,

From it.

From you.

WILD BRUJERIA

I lost my little mountain town,

Sometimes I think I've lost myself, too.

- on running away

Wild Brujeria

I spent my whole life

Having narratives thrust upon me.

Once I finally learned to sing,

I couldn't stop the notes from

Prying open my lips,

  Even if I wanted to.

- songbird

Wild Brujeria

Wild Brujeria

My fingers

Reach for your soul

Scoop stars from your insides

Your body grabs me

Holds me

As we scream in ecstasy

I live there, in that moment,

In that reel

Of what we were

Together

- come with me

Wild Brujeria

Wild Brujeria

So many words

I'd like to say

Instead I'll close my eyes

And let them wash away

- empty lips sink ships

Wild Brujeria

Wild Brujeria

Fighting for my right to life,

Fighting for the truth.

So rude

How they tear me to pieces,

Feed my body back to me

One crumb at a time,

The bastards –

They can't have us.

- on my fourth disability claim denial

Wild Brujeria

Wild Brujeria

"Where are you from?"

They ask me,

Their eyebrows angling, furrowing, trying

To place my Hispanic features and pale skin,

Surely an exotic combination

To them.

I skirt around the question,

Keep skirting,

My skirts flow as I spin round and round,

Spinning up dust,

Dancing with Earth's orbit.

- you cannot name me

Wild Brujeria

Wild Brujeria

Ancestors

Within my very cells

I am everything you are, and are not.

I am everything you could have been, and could not.

I know your suffering

As I know your joy,

Your secrets are held within

Every creaking joint,

Every flutter of lashes,

When I feel so alone, on this desolate plane,

I recall that I am you, again

And I hug myself,

As I imagine you would,

And I honor your secrets

By living them, in the open,

As I'm sure

You wish you could.

- a letter to my ancestors

Wild Brujeria

Wild Brujeria

Living with a vulva

Is like living with a wound

Open and bleeding

Dependent upon the moon

And its stars.

The people of the world

Want nothing more than to pierce us

Over and over.

We bleed and bleed

Until these veins run dry

Like earth's waters

And her breathable sky.

- bleed us dry

Wild Brujeria

Wild Brujeria

You gasp in awe at the thickness of my eye lashes

But retch in disgust when the thickness reaches elsewhere -

Arms, legs, pits, nethers,

Stomach,

Chest,

Sacrum,

You want to cut out pieces of me,

Only keep a few for yourself

Yet in doing so

You steal it all

Away.

- i was born whole

Wild Brujeria

Wild Brujeria

How could I hate my body

When I love every part of Mother Earth?

They say when you die,

You cry out for mother.

I know mine

Will be there to cradle me

One last time.

I know when I cry out,

Mother will answer.

She is ivy in the winter,

Cedarwood in the spring,

She is the very air which I breathe,

And the limbs that hold me up.

When I return to her,

She will receive me

With a kiss.

I have always been

a part of this.

- worthy of tenderness

Wild Brujeria

Wild Brujeria

In the spring,

The flowers bloom.

In autumn,

Mushrooms come.

They hide away,

Then show their face.

Oh dear god,

I love this place.

- always home

Wild Brujeria

Wild Brujeria

My new home is Portland, Oregon

Her Redwoods and Douglas Firs and Western Cedars

Wave their leaves and limbs as I pass,

As if they're saying 'hello'

The trees are friendly

They get quiet when it's dry too long,

But when the air is dripping with moisture and fog,

And the ground beneath is a muddy bog,

The trees like to talk

They therapize me,

A stranger passing through,

As if they know my heart is true

I feel seen here,

In this quiet

My only companions

Are my own two feet

And as I pass,

The willows weep

All too soon

My eyes grow bleary

My limbs grow weary

The trail is narrow,

It climbs the spine of Mother Earth

My unsteady feet

Shuffle over grey stones

I try not to break my bones

I know I must rest,

But where?

The path opens wide,

I feel its maw could swallow me

But there, near the creek, is a boulder

Blanketed in moss

Perfect for sitting

While my eyelids are flitting

I slip,

Then fall into

Sleep

- narcolepsy, the thief

Wild Brujeria

I lay beneath

A redwood tree

At the renaissance faire

The third of three

My friends, you see

Had left me be

Alone,

My head in the sand

The redwood tree

Stayed there for me

And with surprise

I did Arise

Anew,

A narcoleptic warrior.

- narcoleptic warrior

Wild Brujeria

WILD BRUJERIA

Thank you, Mother Moon

for lighting the way.

Thank you, Brother Trees,

for shading the day.

Thank you, Bird Friends,

For your songs of glee,

And thank you for staying,

For hoping,

Me.

- never truly alone

About The Author

Tatiana Maria Corbitt is a Mexican-American mestizo writer and multidisciplinary artist. They graduated summa cum laude with their MS and BS in Applied Biological Sciences from Arizona State University. They now reside in the ethereal Pacific Northwest with their German Shepherd Service Dog. *Wild Brujeria* is Tatiana's first published book of poetry. They can be found on Instagram @authortatianamaria.